Baby

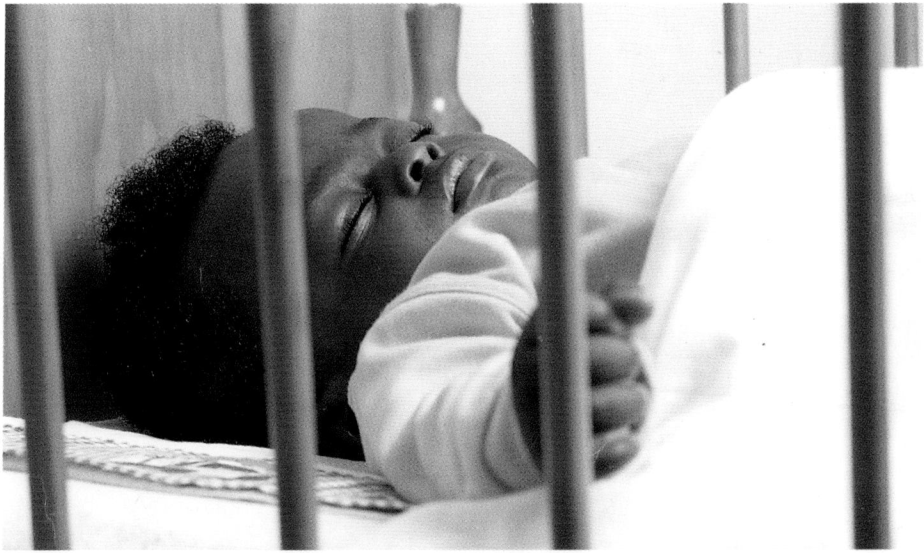

Baby is drinking.

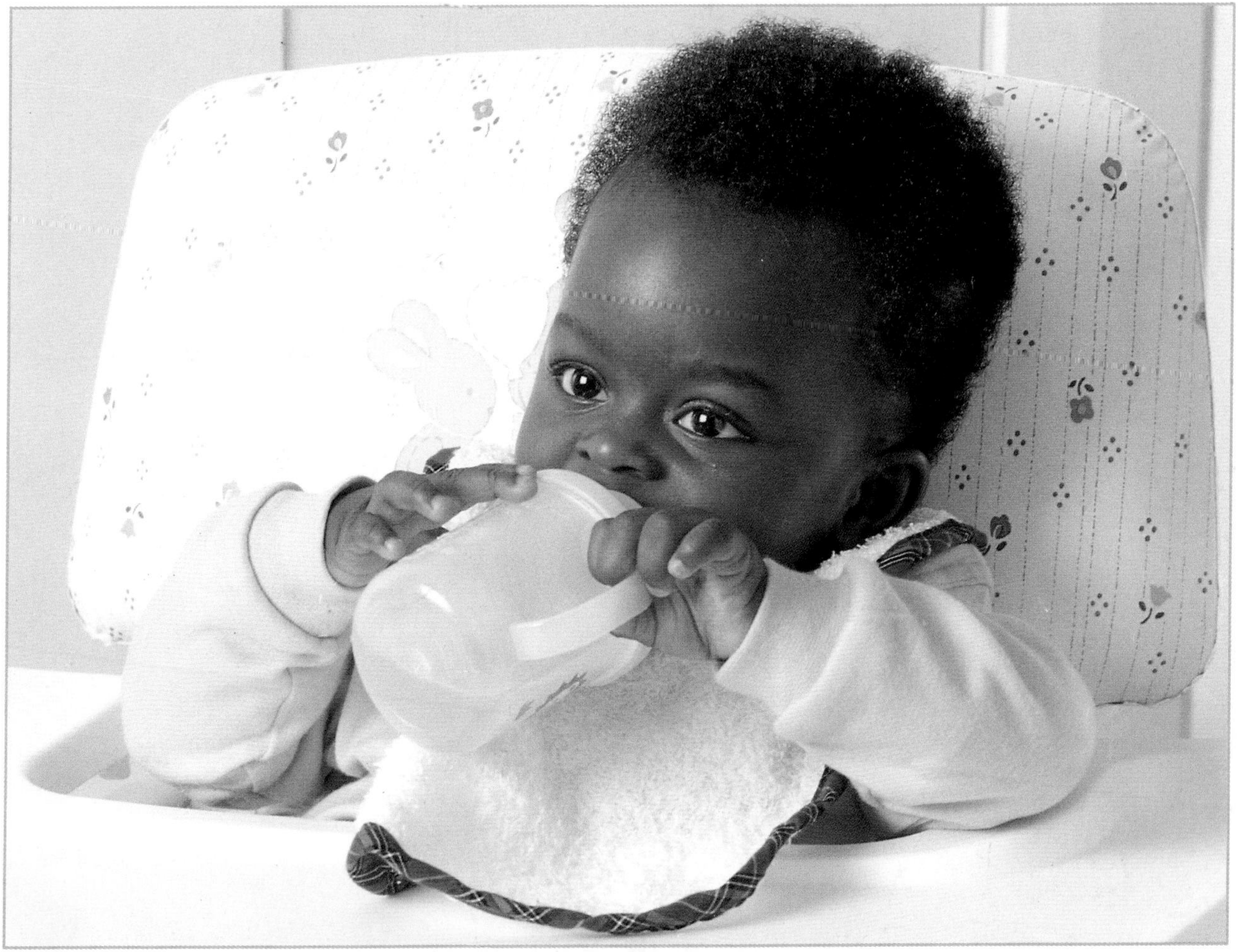

Baby is eating.

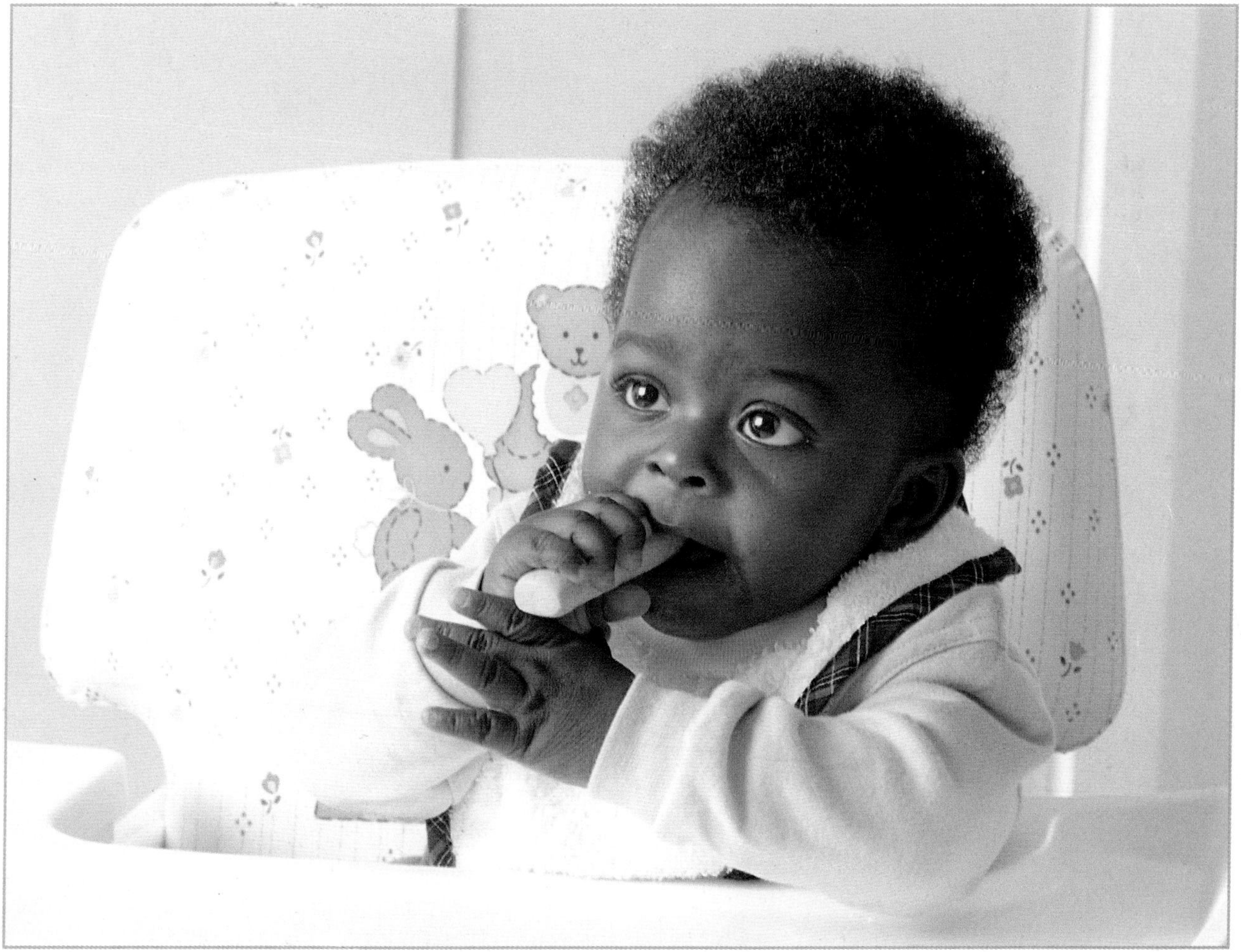

Baby is crawling.

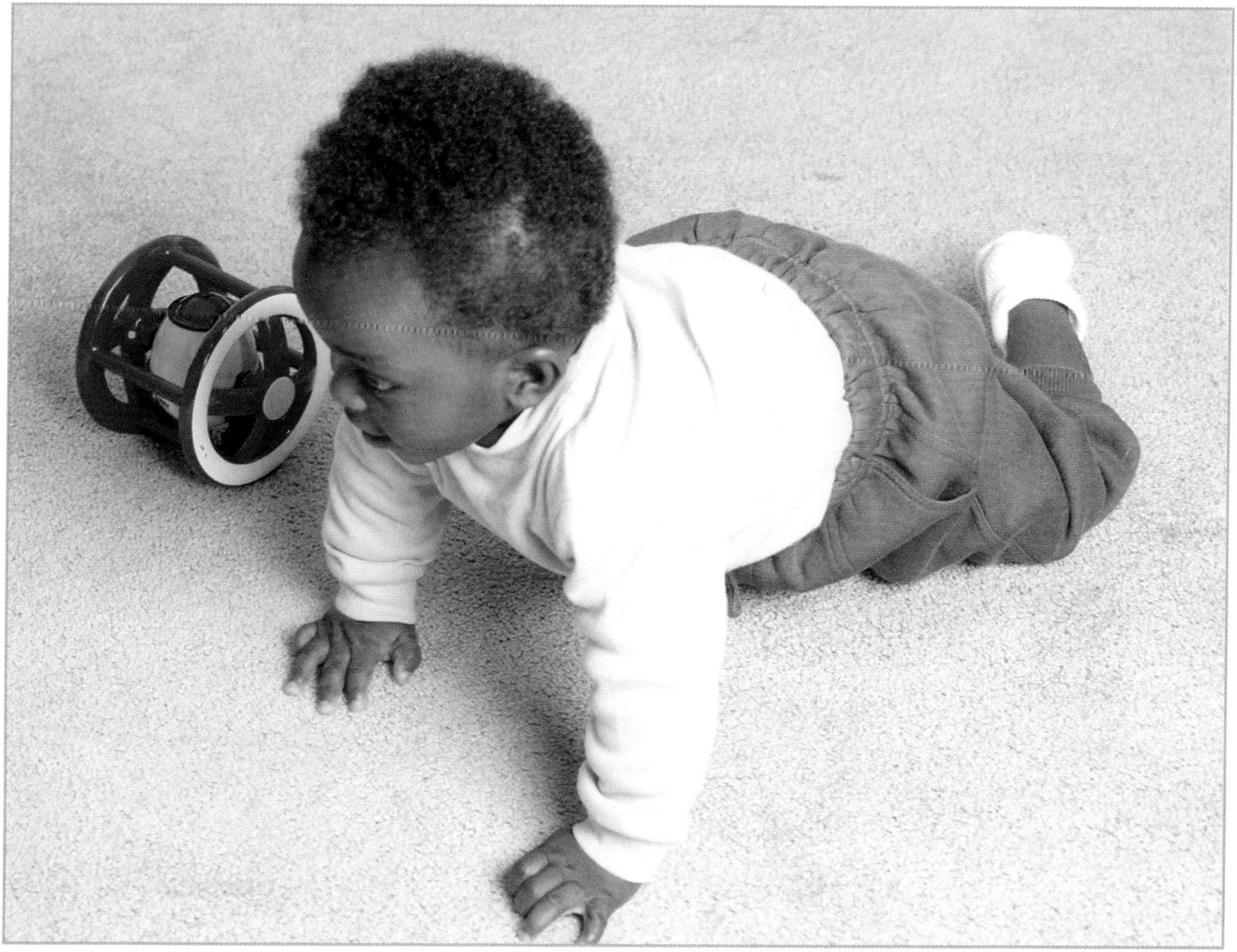

Baby is playing.

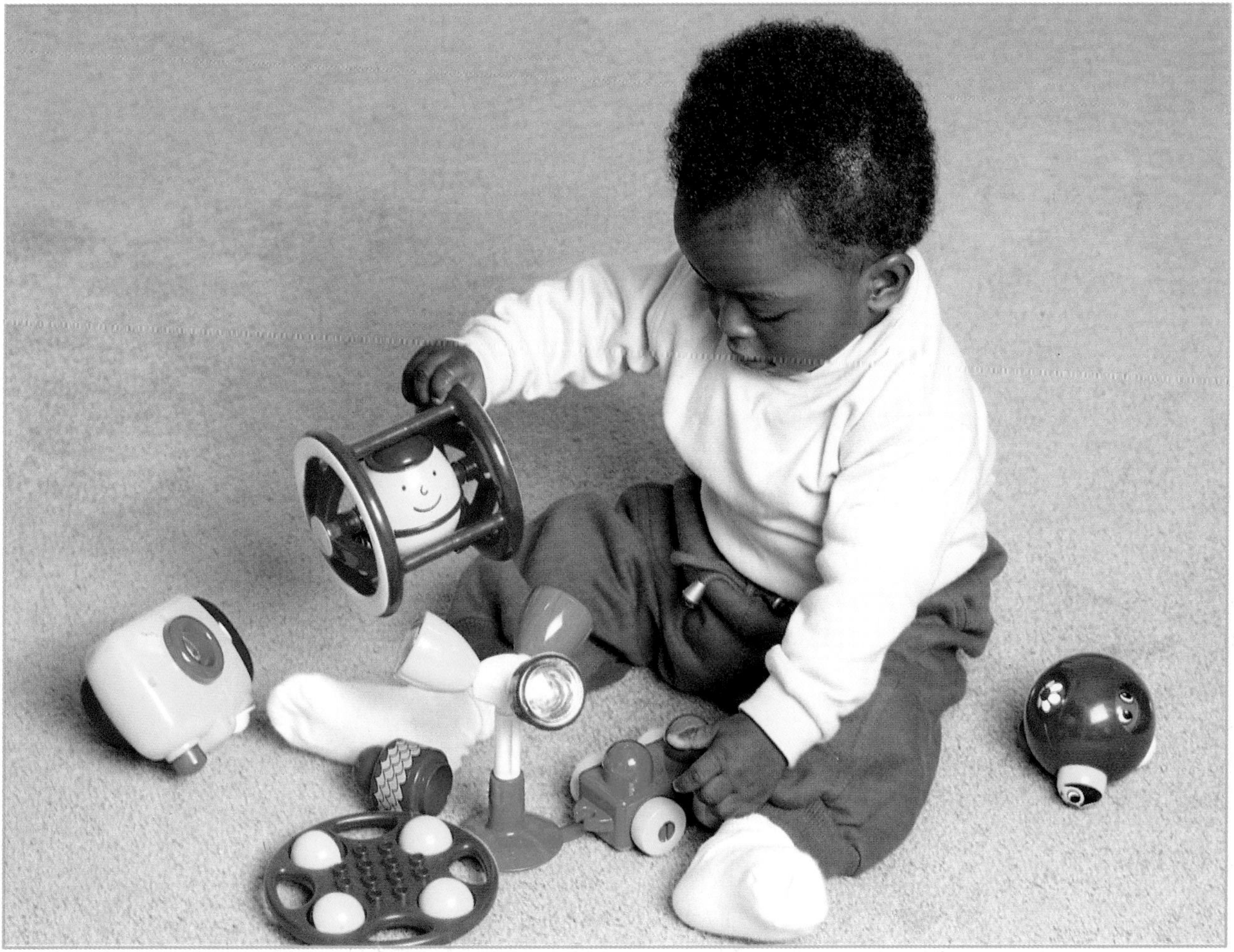

Baby is swinging.

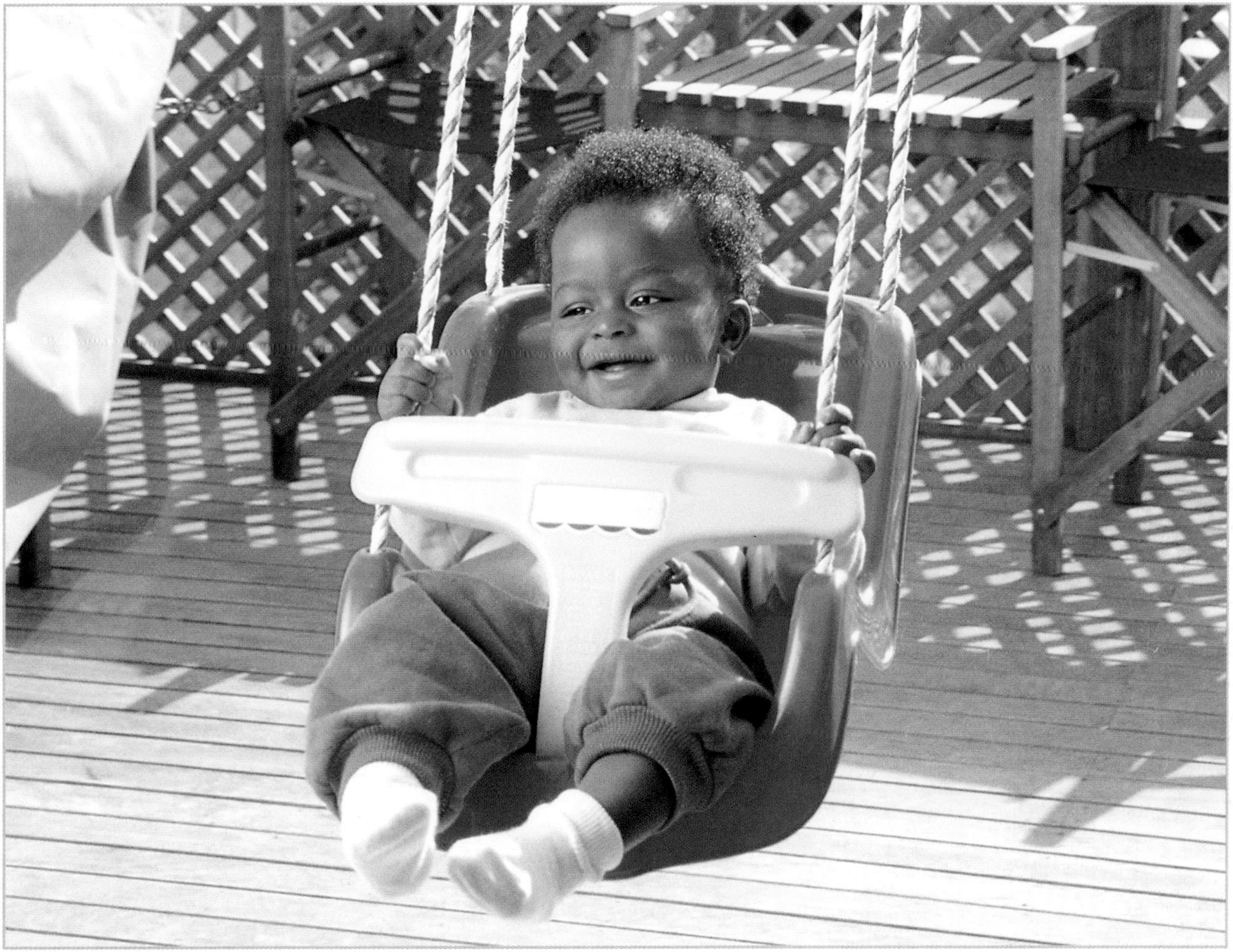

Baby is laughing.

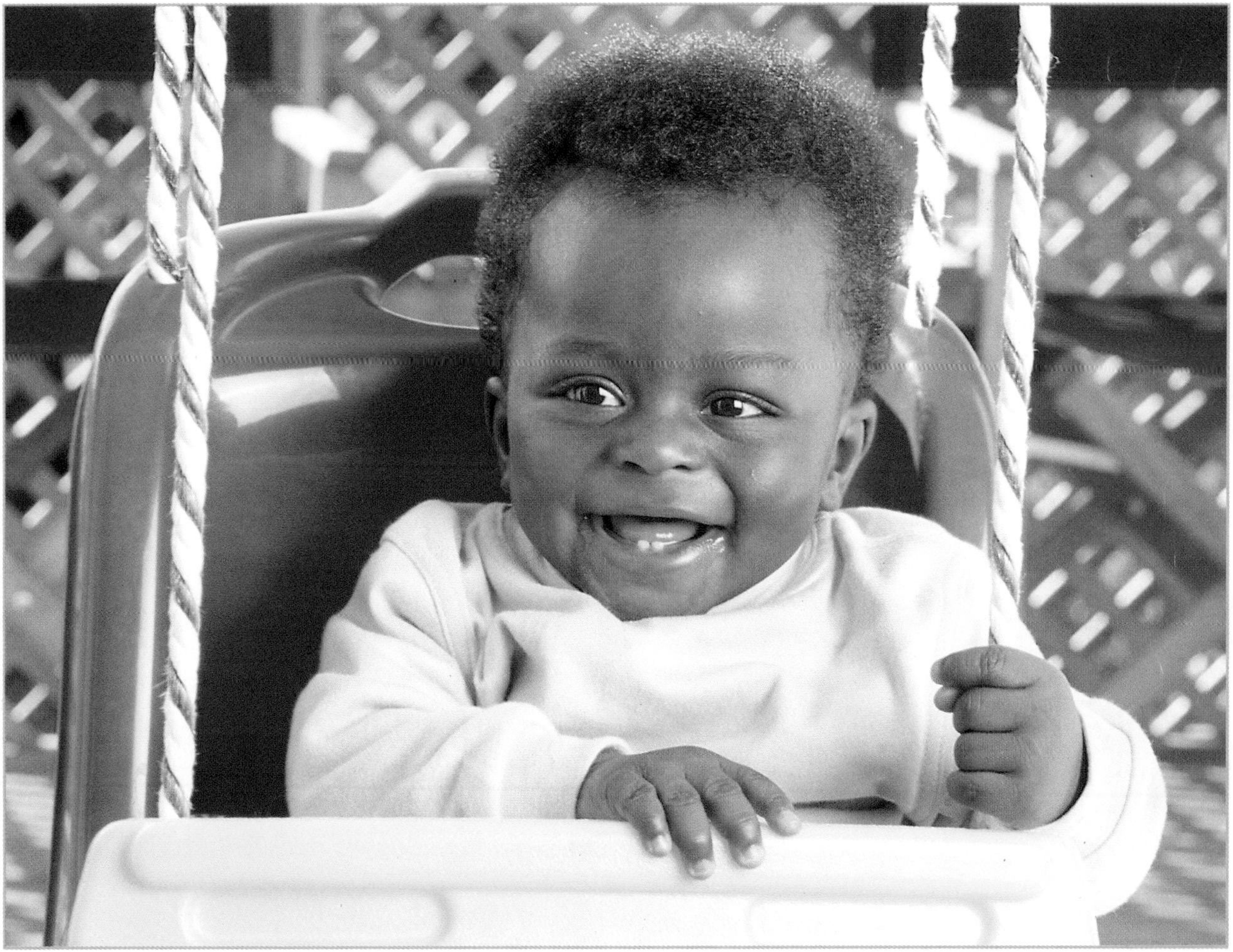

Baby is crying.

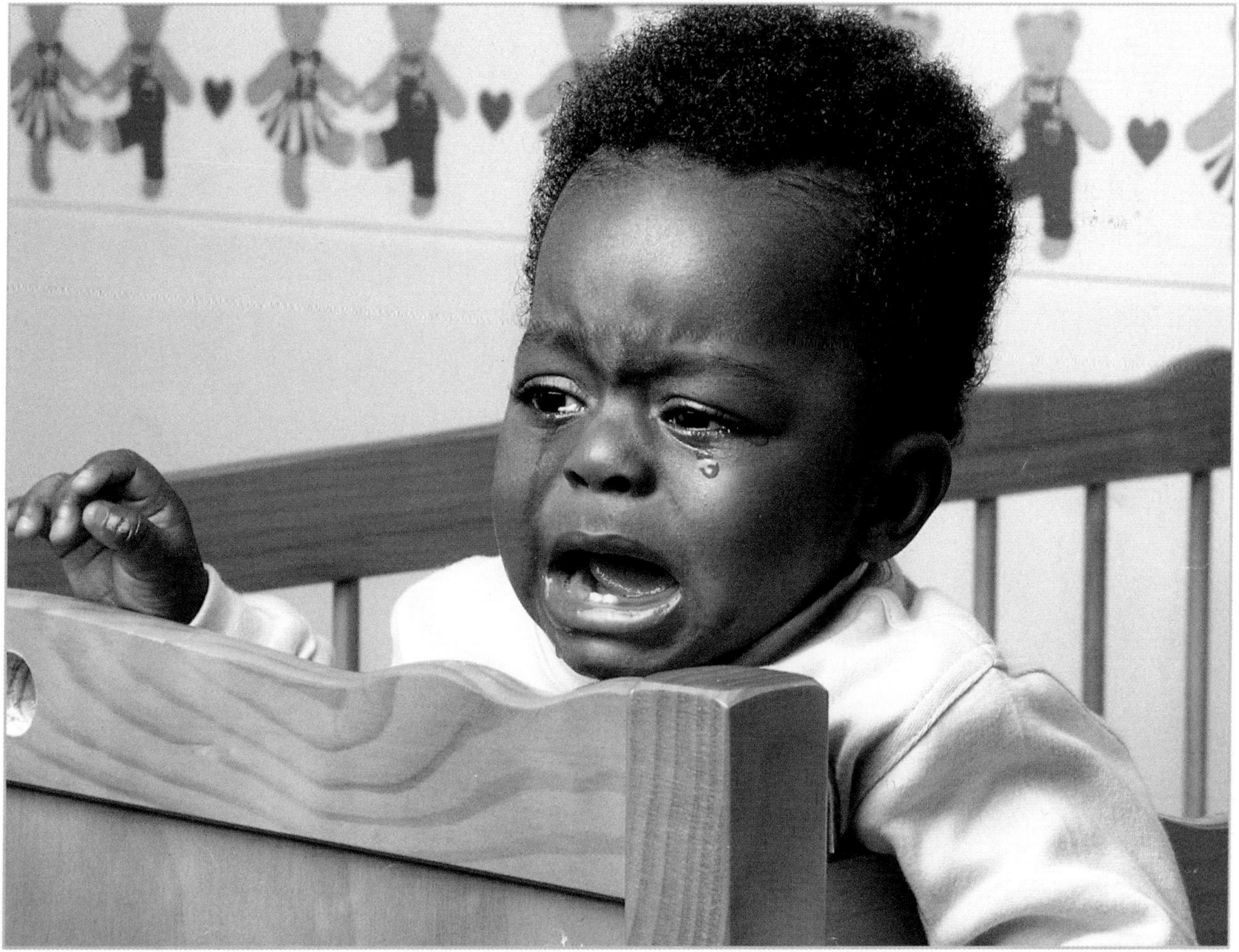

Baby is sleeping.

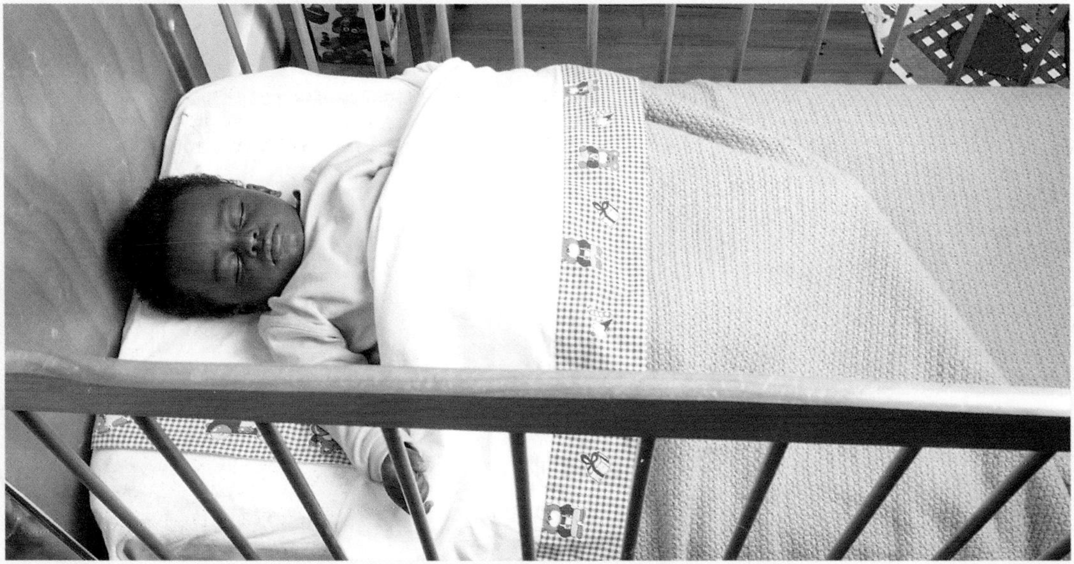